HURTS LIKE A ~~MOTHER~~ *(JEW)* MOTHER

A Cautionary Aleph-Bet

By Ruby Rosen & Rosie Rubin

Illustrated by Gal Weizman

HURTS LIKE A JEWISH MOTHER

Text: Ruby Rosen & Rosie Rubin
Illustrations: Gal Weizman
Cover and Interior Design and Layout: Danielle Smith-Boldt

For more information, please contact:
Mascot Books
620 Herndon Parkway, Suite 320
Herndon, VA 20170
info@mascotbooks.com

www.mascotbooks.com

Library of Congress Control Number: 2021900465

CPSIA Code: PRQ0321A
ISBN-13: 978-1-64543-921-9

Printed in the Malaysia

Abby blew her savings, bankrolling the Bat Mitzvah

Batya was distraught –
her boy dated a Shiksa

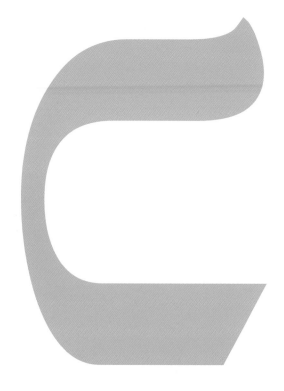

Chava was trampled while dancing the Hora

The Yad speared **D**afna when she read the Torah

Braiding the challah,
Eve tied herself in a knot

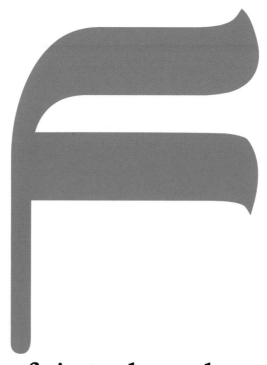

Franny fainted at the party - the cold cuts weren't Glatt!

Gila's knees buckled,
bowing down in the Aleynu

When the wind took **H**annah's wig, she screamed "Dayenu!"

Eating meals in the Sukkah gave **I**lana frostbite

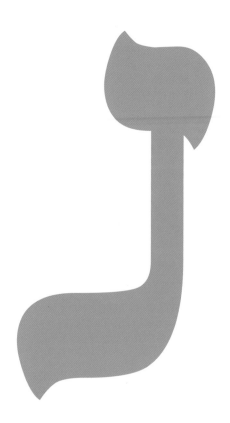

Caught sneaking lobster,
Judith turned ghost-white

While burning the Chametz,
Karen lit up like a spark

Tree-hugging on Tu B'Shevat,
Leah was clawed by the bark

Michal's fingers got stuck on
a Mezuzah that had frozen

Noa's folks sat shiva when she changed her name from Rosen

Ora crashed into a tree,
racing home for candle lighting

Peninah clogged an artery:
the latkes - too inviting!

Queshet was discovered doing laps in the Mikvah

On Purim an errant Gragger
almost impaled **R**ivkah

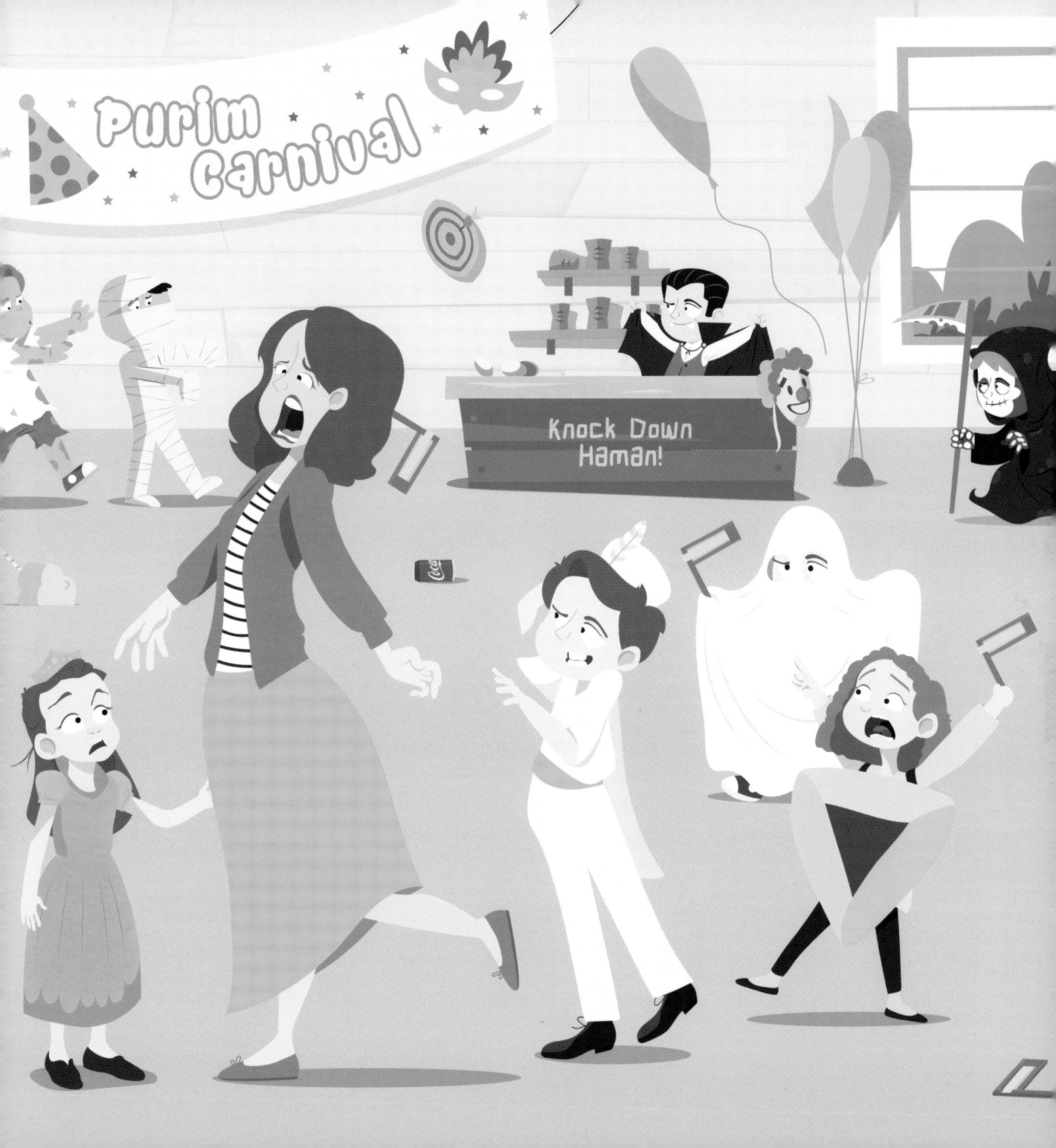

Purim Carnival
Knock Down Haman!

Tikiah Gadola had **S**ara
gasping for air

Hiding the afikoman,
Tal was pinned by the chair

A bird's-eye view at the Bris
left **U**llia aghast

Vered was skin and bones
post-Yom Kippur fast

The rabbi's interminable sermon
knocked **W**endy out cold

The Seder's fourth cup of wine
made **X**enia too bold

Constant Hebrew school
complaints fueled **Y**ael's malaise

Zelda needed extra rest–
she kept Shabbat for days!

About the Authors

Rosie Rubin and Ruby Rosen met in a mikvah waiting room fifteen years ago. This is their first book together. When not arguing about their favorite Jewish rappers, taste-testing wines for the holidays, or highlighting outfits on their fashion blog *Kosher Couture,* Rosie and Ruby are on the stand-up circuit, doing shows to help people appreciate other cultures and religions. Coming soon to a club near you!

About the Illustrator

Gal Weizman is an illustrator and character designer, based in Jerusalem, Israel. Her portfolio showcases her distinctive style across a range of work through various mediums: TV, print and interactive design. She brings her lovely creations to life with simple ideas and characters positioned in strange, funny and touching situations. She has over fifteen books published so far.